Christmas
NOTES

Christmas NOTES

CICO BOOKS

LONDON NEW YORK

Published in 2014 by CICO Books
an imprint of Ryland Peters & Small Ltd
20–21 Jockey's Fields, London WC1R 4BW
519 Broadway, 5th Floor, New York, NY 10012

www.rylandpeters.com

10 9 8 7 6 5 4 3 2 1

Compilation © CICO Books 2014

Design © CICO Books 2014

Illustrations © Corbis

A CIP catalog record for this book is available from
the Library of Congress and the British Library.

ISBN: 978-1-78249-163-7

Designer: Emily Breen

Printed in China

Contents

Introduction

The key to a stress-free Christmas is preparation, and with this journal you can make sure that the festive period comes off without a hitch, by counting down the weeks leading up to Christmas Day itself. Planning ahead will mean you can spend less time worrying, and more time with your friends and family.

When planning your perfect holiday, perhaps the most important thing to do is to make lists—gift lists, Christmas card lists, shopping lists, decorating ideas—there are dedicated pages here for all of the things you need to remember to buy, so that everyone receives something they love, and Christmas dinner is a hit.

Food is such a large part of the holiday, so plan the menus for all your parties and dinners in the Menu Planner section. In the rush to plan the main Christmas Day meal, it is easy to forget to plan for the lighter Christmas Eve and post-Christmas meals. Once you have planned your menus, write out your shopping lists—those that can be purchased well in advance and stored or frozen, and the fresh produce that needs to be bought at short notice. In this way you can make sure that you haven't overlooked any vital ingredient.

It is also important to order your Christmas meat early, especially if you plan to serve a free-range or organic turkey, as these less intensively-reared birds are sold in comparatively fewer numbers. Why not support your local butcher with the meat that you choose to buy this Christmas, and order in advance from them?

The gift list section is perfect for noting down your ideas for what to get your family and friends—just jot down your inspirations whenever they strike. In our digital age, it is highly convenient to order your gifts online, and, as long as you order everything in plenty of time, you may never need to battle the crowds or hurriedly buy gifts at the last minute ever again.

Keep a record of your favorite recipes, plan decorating schemes for your home, and more, with this handy journal, and use it every year until it becomes an indispensable bible for your perfect festive period.

Gift list

Gift list

Name:
....

Gift:
....

Store:
....

Price:
....

Name:
....

Gift:
....

Store:
....

Price:
....

Name:
....

Gift:
....

Store:
....

Price:
....

Name:
....

Gift:
....

Store:
....

Price:
....

Name:
....

Gift:
....

Store:
....

Price:
....

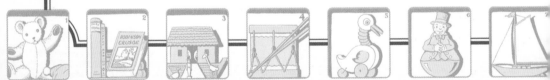

Name:

Gift:

Store:

Price:

Name:

Gift:

Store:

Price:

Name:

Gift:

Store:

Price:

Name:

Gift:

Store:

Price:

Name:

Gift:

Store:

Price:

Gift list

Name:

Gift:

Store:

Price:

Name:

Gift:

Store:

Price:

Name:

Gift:

Store:

Price:

Name:

Gift:

Store:

Price:

Name:

Gift:

Store:

Price:

Name:

Gift:

Store:

Price:

Name:

Gift:

Store:

Price:

Name:

Gift:

Store:

Price:

Name:

Gift:

Store:

Price:

Name:

Gift:

Store:

Price:

Gift list

Name:

Gift:

Store:

Price:

Name:

Gift:

Store:

Price:

Name:

Gift:

Store:

Price:

Name:

Gift:

Store:

Price:

Name:

Gift:

Store:

Price:

Name: ....

Gift: ....

Store: ....

Price: ....

Name: ....

Gift: ....

Store: ....

Price: ....

Name: ....

Gift: ....

Store: ....

Price: ....

Name: ....

Gift: ....

Store: ....

Price: ....

Name: ....

Gift: ....

Store: ....

Price: ....

Gift list

Name:

Gift:

Store:

Price:

Name:

Gift:

Store:

Price:

Name:

Gift:

Store:

Price:

Name:

Gift:

Store:

Price:

Name:

Gift:

Store:

Price:

Name:

Gift:

Store:

Price:

Name:

Gift:

Store:

Price:

Name:

Gift:

Store:

Price:

Name:

Gift:

Store:

Price:

Name:

Gift:

Store:

Price:

4

weeks to go

4 weeks to go

Shopping

This is the best time to take care of shopping that can be done in advance. If you are ordering turkey, game, or any other meat for your main Christmas meal, this is the right time to place your order.

Writing Christmas cards can take longer than expected, so buy them now so you have plenty of time. If you want to make your own cards, buy the card, envelopes, and any decorative touches you may need. If you are sending any cards overseas, check how early they need to be posted.

Stock up with all the dried, tinned, and packet ingredients that you will need over the holidays.

Here is a guide for the ingredients you can buy four weeks in advance, use the blank lined pages that follow to make your own lists:

bread mix

breakfast cereals

cake decorations

cornflour

chips (crisps), olives, and other snacks

essences and flavorings, such as vanilla and almond

flour: self-rising, all-purpose (plain), and wholemeal

jams and jellies

mustard

nuts

oils

dried pasta

pulses

rice

spices

salt and sugar

Cooking

Start cooking dishes that can be put in the freezer, such as pastry, soups, and sauces.

Decorating

Start thinking about how you are going to decorate your home. Look at magazines for inspiration, or at store windows, which are always full of ideas for how to decorate your tree, table, and porch.

If you plan to make your own decorations; here are some useful things to have on-hand:

decorative papers	ribbons
double-sided tape	scissors
fabric paints	spray glue
glitter	stamps
glue	stencils
gold and silver pens and spray paints	sticky tape
	twines

For the freezer

For the freezer

For the store cupboard

For the store cupboard

Drinks

Drinks

3
weeks to go

3 weeks to go

Shopping

Since you purchased all your store-cupboard and freezer essentials last week, you can concentrate on non-food shopping this week. Below is a list of items you might want to consider.

This is also a good time to order gifts online, as they will have plenty of time to arrive before Christmas.

If you need to post any gifts overseas, now is the best time to do so.

aluminum (aluminium) foil (wide enough for your turkey)

baby food

baking parchment

batteries

candles

cards

Christmas crackers

cocktail sticks

cookie cutters in festive shapes

garbage bags

freezer bags

fuses

matches

paper towels, napkins, plates, and cups

paper tablecloths

spare light bulbs

Cooking

Edible gifts are a wonderful idea—to save you the stress of having to make them nearer to Christmas look for ideas that will keep well in jars, like pickles, jellies, and jams, or items such as chocolates that can survive a few weeks in the refrigerator.

Decorating

Check your Christmas tree lights this week and replace them if they no longer work.

Start refining your plans for decorating your home, so you have the time to search for any special items such as candles in a particular color.

2
weeks to go

2 weeks to go

Shopping

Now it is time to turn your mind to the drinks that you will need to buy for the holiday period.

When choosing your wines, try to think about the flavors that will be dominant in the meals you are planning. The rich, spicy trimmings that are served with turkey can dominate classic French wines such as claret and burgundy, so it would be better to choose a Californian Cabernet Sauvignon or a Chilean Cabernet.

When buying low-alcohol wine or beer, check the labeling carefully to make sure you are purchasing exactly what you want.

If storing all these large bottles and boxes is a problem, put them outside the back door, if you are sure they won't disappear. However, beware of frost at night which can make bottles explode!

beer

soft drinks

fruit juices

mineral water

mixers: such as ginger ale, soda water, and tonic water

spirits: such as brandy, port, rum, gin, and whiskey

wines: low-alcohol, red, sparkling, white, and champagne

Cooking

This is the best time to make all remaining food that will freeze well, so that you won't be so pressed for time in the few days before Christmas.

Decorating

Start wrapping your Christmas presents. This can take a long time so it's a task that's best not left until the last moment.

Find and check your Christmas tree decorations. You checked your lights last week but this week is a good time to check that glass decorations have survived a year of storage, and if necessary, to buy some more.

You could also check that all the tablecloths and napkins you will need are clean and well-pressed.

1

week to go

1 week to go

Shopping

Buy any flowers and foliage that you need for the table centerpiece or other arrangements you are considering. Don't leave this too late or stores could sell out.

Also, buy any florist's foam that you may need. This is available as bricks, balls, or wreaths so decide on your requirements before purchasing.

Bring in your Christmas tree from the garden or buy one. If you have the space in your garden to grow a tree, consider buying one with a root ball.

To prevent too many last-minute panics, buy what you need from the following—these items should all keep for a week or more:

bacon

cookies and crackers

cheese

chocolates

coffee/tea, plus filter papers, if necessary

bread: ready to bake or fresh for freezer storage

eggs

nuts

yogurt

Decorating

Everyone has a personal preference over when they like to decorate their tree and house, some people like to leave it as late as Christmas Eve, whereas others start decorating up to three weeks before the big day so they can enjoy their decorations for longer. Plan your decorating schemes on the pages that follow.

Bring out the lights and decorations and have fun with your family as you decorate the tree. Making your own decorations, both edible and not, is a fun activity if you have children.

Make a wreath for your front door!

Decorating ideas

Picture of your decorations

Decorating ideas

....
....
....
....
....
....
....
....

Picture of your decorations

....
....
....
....
....
....
....
....

Decorating ideas

Decorating ideas

Decorating ideas

Decorating ideas

Decorating ideas

2

days to go

2 days to go

Shopping

This is the time to buy your fresh fruit and vegetables! Start shopping early in the day so that you have plenty to choose from in the supermarket. At home, store your purchases in a cool, but frost-free place. Keep potatoes in a dark place or they will turn green.

When buying your vegetables, plan for approximately 4 oz (125 g) per person for each meal.

If you have ordered turkey/game, or another joint of meat, don't forget to pick it up and then keep it in as cool a place as possible.

Some items you may think about buying:

cream

fresh bread

fresh fruit juices

fruit

milk

sausages

vegetables

Cooking

If your meat is frozen, remove it from the freezer and keep it somewhere cool while it thaws.

Check on the length of time you will need to cook the meat so you know how far in advance you will need to make the stuffing.

Decorating

Make your floral table centerpiece and any other arrangements. If you are using florist's foam, don't forget to soak it in advance of making the arrangement.

If your dining table is in a separate room that won't be disturbed before Christmas Day, consider laying it now. If not today, do it on Christmas Eve so you can forget about it.

Christmas crafts and decorating

The tree

The tree

Tabletops and mantelpieces

Tabletops and mantelpieces

The garden

The garden

Making decorations

Making decorations

Inspiration and ideas

Inspiration and ideas

Menu planner

Menu

Date:

Meal:

Guests:

Starter:

Main course:

Dessert:

Cheese:

Drinks:

Shopping list

Menu

Date:

Meal:

Guests:

Starter:

Main course:

Dessert:

Cheese:

Drinks:

Shopping list

Menu

Date:

Meal:

Guests:

Starter:

Main course:

Dessert:

Cheese:

Drinks:

Shopping list

Menu

Date:

Meal:

Guests:

Starter:

Main course:

Dessert:

Cheese:

Drinks:

Shopping list

Menu

Date:

Meal:

Guests:

Starter:

Main course:

Dessert:

Cheese:

Drinks:

Shopping list

Menu

Date:

Meal:

Guests:

Starter:

Main course:

Dessert:

Cheese:

Drinks:

Shopping list

Menu

Date:

Meal:

Guests:

Starter:

Main course:

Dessert:

Cheese:

Drinks:

Shopping list

Menu

Date:

Meal:

Guests:

Starter:

Main course:

Dessert:

Cheese:

Drinks:

Shopping list

Keeping organized

Notes and ideas

Notes and ideas

Notes and ideas

Notes and ideas

Notes and ideas

Notes and ideas

Notes and ideas

Notes and ideas

Notes and ideas

Notes and ideas

Notes and ideas

Notes and ideas

Notes and ideas

Notes and ideas

Notes and ideas

Notes and ideas

Notes and ideas

Notes and ideas

Notes and ideas